a visit to the DAIRY FARM

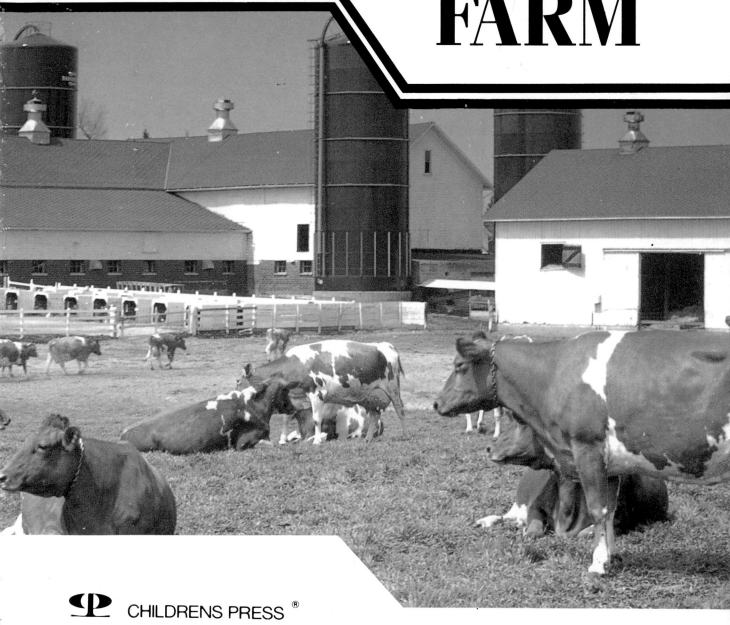

CHILDRENS PRESS ®

CHICAGO

by Sandra Ziegler

With appreciation to the HOARD'S DAIRYMAN FARM, Fort Atkinson, Wisconsin, for cooperation in the photographing of this book.

Appreciation is also expressed to the children from TEACHING CENTERS, Milwaukee, Wisconsin, who worked with us so patiently as we recorded their visit to the dairy farm on film.

Photography by PILOT PRODUCTIONS, INC.
   Dave Holmes, photographer
   Jay Kelly, lighting assistant
   Dean Garrison, director

Photos on cover and pages 1, 4 (bottom), 8, 9, 12, 13, 14 (bottom), 16 (top), 28, and 30 courtesy of *Hoard's Dairyman—The National Dairy Farm Magazine*, James S. Baird—Art Director.

Photos on pages 19 (bottom), 21, 22, 24, and 26 (right) courtesy of Wisconsin Dairies Cooperative.

Photo on page 31 courtesy of Wisconsin Milk Marketing Board.

Library of Congress Cataloging-in-Publication Data

Ziegler, Sandra 1938-
   A visit to the dairy farm / by Sandra Ziegler; (created by the Child's World).
      p.   cm. — (Field trip books)
   Summary: A class visits a large dairy farm and sees the animals and activities to be found there.
   ISBN 0-516-01496-X
   1. Dairy farming—Juvenile literature.   2. Farm life—Juvenile literature.   3. Dairy farms—Wisconsin—Fort Atkinson—Juvenile literature.   [1. Dairying.   2. Farm life.]   I. Child's World (Firm)   II. Title.   III. Series: Field trip series.
SF239.5.Z54   1987   87-19692
637—dc19   CIP

1 2 3 4 5 6 7 8 9 10 11 12 R 95 94 93 92 91 90 89 88 87

a visit to the DAIRY FARM

Created by The Child's World

"Hello," says Mrs. Dolan. "Welcome to the dairy farm. Kathy has been wanting you to visit."

Kathy's class is happy to be at the farm. They want to learn all about it.

"What shall we see first, Mom?" asks Kathy.

"I saw some cows by the barn as we came up the road," says Tommy.

"Let's look at them first," says Mrs. Dolan. The teacher, Mrs. Payne, agrees.

As the children look at the cows, Mrs.
Dolan says, "Most of our cows have calves
every year. These cows will have calves
soon."

"Don't you have any calves now?" Greg
asks.

"Yes, we do," Mrs. Dolan says. "Would
you like to see them next?"

"Yes," says Greg.

Mrs. Dolan leads the children into a special part of the barn. There they meet the newest member of the dairy herd. Her mother is giving her a bath.

"When she gets bigger," Mrs. Dolan says, "she will have her own house outside.

"Each older calf has its own house, called
a calf hutch. A calf lives in its hutch until it
is three months old. Inside the hutch is hay
for the calf to eat.

Pam pets a calf. The calf nibbles at her fingers.

Mrs. Dolan says that it is time for the calf to eat. The calf wants something more than just hay. She wants a bottle of milk.

Soon Mr. Dolan comes. He gives each calf a big baby bottle. The children pet the calves as they watch them eat.

Some think petting the calves is fun. But others aren't so sure.

The children visit more grown-up cows
next. They are eating hay.

"When it is shivery cold outside, the
cows eat inside the barn," Mrs. Dolan says.
The children like that idea a lot.

"We grow most of the food for our cows," Mr. Dolan says. "And we keep it in the big, blue silos. We also buy them some special food. We call it 'cow chow.'"

The children learn that along with hay and "cow chow," the cows also eat corn silage. It is made of corn and chopped-up corn plants. Mr. Dolan shows them a handful. The children can see the corn in it. Can you?

"What shall we see next?" Mrs. Dolan asks the class.

"The heifer barn," Kathy says.

"What is a heifer?" Brian asks.

"It's a cow that is bigger than a calf but smaller than a mama cow," Mrs. Dolan says. "A heifer is a cow that hasn't had a calf yet, so it isn't old enough to milk."

15

The heifer barn doesn't look like a "real" barn. Kathy says it is open on the side so that the sun can shine in and help keep the young cows warm on cold, winter days.

As the children stand by the fence, the curious cows come to look at them.

"It is time to milk," Mrs. Dolan says, "so let's visit the milking barn."

On the way, the children stop to pet one of Kathy's kittens.

The cows are already inside when the children get to the milking barn. Jenny wishes aloud that the cows had hay to eat. But Mr. Dolan says that the cows would rather eat outside on such a nice day.

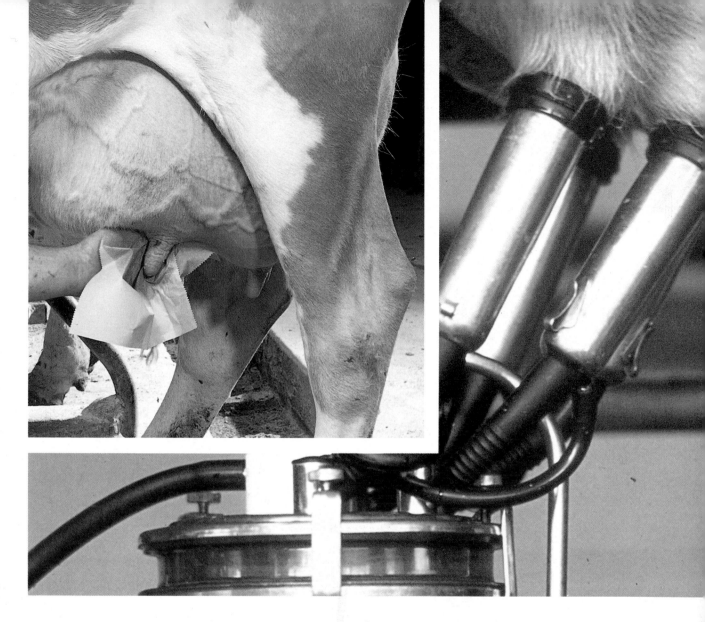

Mr. Dolan cleans each cow and checks her milk. Then he uses a machine to do the milking. He can milk three cows at the same time.

He tells the children that there are ninety cows to milk. "Our cows are milked every morning and every night," he says.

"See the milk," says Mrs. Dolan.

As the children watch, milk splashes about inside the milking machine. Then it runs into a hose and up to a pipe above. It's on its way to the milk room.

In the milk room, the children see a big, round, glass ball.

The milk splashes around inside and fills the ball. Then a pump turns on. It pumps the milk from the ball into a milk tank.

The only way to see the milk inside the big tank is to climb up a ladder and look in a hole on the top. The children don't look. They just imagine the milk inside.

Outside again, Kathy says, "Look, Mom, the milk truck is coming to pick up our milk."

"Yes," says Mrs. Dolan. "Let's move so the truck can get by."

Kathy waves to the driver as the truck passes. He comes to their farm every other day, so he knows Kathy.

Then Tommy wants to see the tractors. So
Mrs. Dolan lets the children see a big one
and. . .

a little one. Jenny is the first to sit on the
little tractor. Jon is next.

A hay wagon is near the tractor, so the children explore it too. They think it is fun to sit on the fresh hay.

"Sometimes we go on hay rides," says Kathy. "The little tractor pulls the wagon." The children think that would be fun.

Finally, Mrs. Payne says that they must start for the bus. It is time for them to leave.

"I think the cows know we are leaving," Jon says, as they pass some cows. "I think they will miss us."

"I'm glad you came to visit us," says Mrs. Dolan.

"We're glad we came too," say the children. "Thank-you for inviting us."

"Good-by, cows," says Beth, as she looks back at the farm from the bus window.

"I like the farm," Jon says. "Maybe I'll be a farmer when I get big."

Back at school, Mrs. Payne shows the
children a picture. "Here are some things
we get from milk," she says.

Can you think of others?